BUTTERFLIES FOR BREAKFAST?

AF614142

first published 2009

© Ian Beckett 2009

for all my family and friends

who have been the inspiration for these verses.

ian@beckett.ie

ISBN: 978-1-4452-0961-6

BUTTERFLIES FOR BREAKFAST?

BUTTERFLIES

FOR

BREAKFAST?

RED HOT SUMMER

Too hot for eating
Too hot for drinking
Too hot for thinking

Too hot for hugging
Too hot for kissing
Too hot for loving

Too hot for not

Too hot for shirt
Too hot for trousers
Too hot for almost anything

Too hot together in coldlicious shared shower
Too hot to stay cool as our temperatures rise

Too hot as ice-cold razors of water turn to steam

Too hot for hot.

BUTTERFLIES FOR BREAKFAST?

Butterflies before you sit the final exam,

Butterflies before you go for a job interview,

Butterflies before you ask her out on a date,

Butterflies before you kiss her for the first time,

Butterflies before you propose two will be one,

Butterflies before you meet her family,

Butterflies before you see her all in white,

Butterflies before you make that big speech,

Butterflies before you see that your baby is OK,

Butterflies before you get news from the doctor,

Butterflies before you lose your job again,

Butterflies before you face any little crisis,

But -

No butterflies for breakfast.

LITTLE THINGS

The hello again smile whenever I arrive home,
A welcome hug when I feel you in my arms,
The want you now look in a crowded room,
A want you back when I am going on a trip,
The sleepy smile as I leave you alone in bed,
A hope you have fun with our boys goodbye.

The holding hands as we walk on the beach,
A million Little Things in our lifetime together,
The no regrets ever as my heart beats fast,
A comfortable cuddle as we drift off to sleep,
The spring in your step after a sleep-in morning,
A closeness with the other half of me - with me.

BLUE HORIZON

Woke up this morning feeling empty,

Faster than fire, slower than standing,

So far from home on this endless road.

Blue horizon slices this workday dawn,

Vapour vortex trails my hellish journey,

Living in very long seconds on this plane.

Hours to go before I sleep with you again.

DROWNING IN YOUR EYES

Sea rolls darkly in timeless silence,

Salt waves foam in endless harmony.

Drowning in your liquid eyes tonight,

Dreaming I feel the touch of your love,

Your soft warm body curling around me,

Sensuous darkness of living in your love.

Hearts and waves beat in synchronicity.

PENNIES

Paper sharp cut,

Slices deep,

Painless initially,

Blood bright red,

Flows freely,

Stings like nettle,

Finger sucking sore,

Bitter metallic,

Tingles strangely,

Japan flag tissue,

Stiffens sore,

Memory tricks,

Taste pennies,

Flashes of childhood.

THE FINAL JOURNEY

I was very
Close to death today,
On the road to Cochabamba.
The "too many" sad lines of crosses,
None of them planned to die.
How can you know?
How will I know?
When?
I live each day
As if it is my last,
So that,
When
I come
to the end
of the road,
Unfulfilled desires,
Will not torment me
In the next life, if there is one.

EL VIAJE FINAL

Yo estaba muy
cerca de la muerte hoy,
en el camino a Cochabamba.
Las "muchas" líneas de cruces tristes,
ninguna de ellas previsto para morir.
¿Cómo puede usted saber?
¿Cómo saber?
¿Cuándo?
Yo vivo cada día
como si fuera mi último.
Así que
cuándo
llegue
al final
del camino,
deseos incumplidos,
no me atormentarán
en la vida próxima, si hay una.

SUICIDE

I feel bleaker than bleak

More empty than full
More restless than calm
More hopeless than hard
More gutless than strong
More boneless than brave
More pointless than sharp
More faceless than feared
More skinless than naked
More airless than breath
More lifeless than dead
More useless than you

I feel like crying inside.

Won't someone just do something?

WHEN I DIE

My

Love,

When I die,

Wear a happy face,

Even though you may be crying inside.

You were my up, my down, my going in, my coming out.

You made me often happy and sometimes sad.

You were the life of my love,

You were my home,

Coming home

To.

PRISON

If you feel imprisioned today,
In factory, office, school,
With woman, parent, child,
Just the groundhog day of life.

These words can set you free
From your private prison cell –

You can walk along the shore,
With sand between your toes,
And salt-caked cracking lips.

You can fly a million miles,
With sea below and stars above,
And wind-watered streaming eyes.

You can be your inner self,
With dreams and touch of love,
And razor-sharp passions edge.

Let the inspiration of my words be
Like the rumble of a small earthquake,
Or the flash of lightning thunder,
In the whirlwind of your future.

You can ....

FORGETTING

Love is so easy, forgetting is so hard.
I remember every moment I am alone
With you in the companionship of silence.
What do you think, where will I go now?
Staring into the blue ocean of your eyes.

Love is so short, forgetting is so long.
I remember every inch of you in my dreams
Without you in my empty room tonight.
What do you dream, where do you go now?
Staring at two ceilings across two oceans.

Love is so full, forgetting is so empty.
I remember your every electric touch,
Without you my world could not turn.
What do you feel, where do we go now?
Staring at the deep ocean of our love.

REMEMBERING

Love is so easy, remembering is so good.
I forget the world every time I am alone
With you in the companionship of silence.
What do you think, where will I go now?
Staring into the blue ocean of your eyes.

Love is so short, remembering is so sharp.
I forget everything but you in my dreams
Without you in my empty room tonight.
What do you dream, where do you go now?
Staring at two ceilings across two oceans.

Love is so full, remembering is so complete.
I forget all but your gentle magic touch,
Without you my world could not turn.
What do you feel, where do we go now?
Staring at the deep ocean of our love.

TIME & DISTANCE

The time when the fire of love,
Becomes the warmth of loving,
When the electricity of touch,
Becomes the comfort of a hug,
When the pleasure of passion,
Becomes the marriage of minds,
When the frustration of routine,
Becomes the wish of escape,
When the distance of absence,
Becomes the need of closeness,
When the freedom of together,
Becomes the perfection of us.

CHISINAU

Slendiforous girls in their sexy summer clothes,
Their stilettos strutter on the sticky hot streets,
Knowing you are distractible by catwalk curves,
The streets a clutteration of Volgas and Volvos.

Breakfast harpist plays muzak in the morning,
Makes my ham and eggs strangely indigestible,
And lobby designer shops jarringly bankrupt,
Tartan uniforms match carpet in the "Irish" bar.

Just another comfortabulous hotel home, again.

MAGIC MADRID

So near, but twenty years is so long ago,
Iberia struggle of that old Wescan show,
Road from the airport is a motorway now.

The Fuente de Neptuno at Palace Hotel,
Warm comfort of a Heavenly bed is swell,
As the cars pass the trident driving like hell.

Lovely to see old friends of Madrid again,
Late night dinner of langostino al ajillo then,
Cafe solo memories writing the trip's amen.

I wait for Aer Lingus, the flight has in-flown,
More magic moments flying Over the Town,
Heading home to my Dublin touch-down.

ALAN

I have Uptown Girl on my DVD,
And Friends on the floor,
I am moving to the music,
And rocking to the beat.

I have training centre every day,
And I am working very hard,
I know that I am growing up,
Everyone tells me so.

I am at Bayside Gym each week,
And have won a lot of medals,
I got them at gymnastics events,
In Dublin , Belfast and Milan.

I go to movies every Saturday,
And eat in Eddie Rocket's,
I like my dad to come along,
And share my coke and popcorn.

I love my mum and dad a lot,
And brothers John & Steve,
I know they are so proud of me,
Everything I do and am.

I pour my milk into a glass,
And cook waffles for a snack,
I hope you like this little note,
And that's all I have to say.

FATHER

He had sunken, slightly disappointed, kind eyes,

Illness barely gave him 3 score years and 10.

He always expected that God would intervene,

To prevent business failure after Biblical 40 years.

Trusting faithfully to the end – a gentle man.

"Look after your Mother" – his last words to me.

TEMPTING

It's five in the morning and five legs from La Paz,
Leaving you is so hard to do these days,
Vienna apartment bed is too tempting and warm.
Lufthansa to London is ice cold Teutonic charm,
Followed by an endless walk in terminal three.

A cosmopolitan coagulated soup of human cargo,
Onomatopoeia of Chicoutimi en route to Chicago,
In "The Bank Job" bad guys got away - that's new.
Then it's First to Miami and missionaries on 922,
Dowdily intent on saving souls in the land of coca.

It's five in the morning again in airless El Alto at last,
A million peasants to save and salteña for breakfast,
Good for me that they all still need to call for advice,
To say "Hi", "Bye" and "Why?" in this socialist paradise,
The challenge of change and the pursuit of profit.

RAIN

Is a pain
When playing

Is expected
When rocking

Is wanted
When sowing

Is a menace
When parading

Is too much
When holidaying

Is too little
When deserting

Is amazing
When lightning

Is angry
When thundering

Is just right
When at night.

SWEAT

I am running quickly down the street,
I smile "Hello" at everyone I meet,
I window startled see a naked me,
I ask what why and how can this me be?

I stop I stare and everyone is laughing,
I see my startled staff and bosses pointing,
I cannot move but then I start to tumble,
I wake alert, cold sweat and all a jumble.

HILTON HOTEL

Madrid Hilton at 40C feels like hell,

A dry emptiness in a hot new hotel,

Inside is black and white and bare,

Greene and style meet in the atrium,

Tonight it's "The power and the Glory",

Next table girl "Blackberries" everyone,

The loneliness of travelling alone,

The reason for a mobile phone.

IN VINO VERITAS

Dos cervezas por favor in De K'ffe,
Cold bite of the first beer refreshes.
Una mas and workday fades to dull,
The night feels bright and hopeful,
The Palitos de pollo satisfies hunger.
Conversation flows to Cepas de Altura,
Three bottles later the stories repeat,
Groundhog day of interesting lives,
With eternal friendship in every bottle.
Six corks line up like truth bullets,
In an aggression of arguments,
Maybe he has just said too much,
Friendship of an unremembered hug,
Next day sorry and failings forgotten.

LAUNCH

Living
On the edge
Of adrenaline
With caffeine
No sleep.

Torture team
Manage manager
Calm customers
Shoot supplier
No sleep.

Fixes fail
Skype saviour
Possible plan
Fanatic focus
No sleep.

Forget food
More madness
Temper tantrum
Solution soon
No sleep

Rock & roll
Back broken
Problem past
Adrenaline addict
No sleep

Go to bed – write this poem.

GIVING

Living
Is giving
All of you,
In lots of
Little pieces.

Until you feel
Empty – then,
Something
Happens.

You start
To feel,
Alive.

REALITY TV

Dinner, Dafney hot, courtyard cool and civilized,
Fettuccini fabulous, guest glamorous and glowing,
Eyes starlike smiling, pulpo carpaccio savoured.

Reality will bite in next week's jungle game.
Imagination runs riot, perfect picture of dinner
For ants, ambling in forbidden places, ouch.

Coiffeurless, bad-hair-day, dishevelled demon,
Boredom, book, arachnophobia perhaps, escape.
Red carpet missed, pampering needed, tranquilo.

MEETING FOR LUNCH

Good friends meet again for a lunch-time chat,
We wonder what we have all been at.
Luxor cruise luxury of mummy-less magic,
Santiago by bus for a friend's welcome back.
The world of a "dry" poet surprises the clique.
Dürnstein weekend seems rather prosaic.

Absent friends are also at the lunch-time chat,
We wonder what they have all been at.
Escape from girlfriends, only to end up in the pot,
Not sure whether he is worried or not.
Another has fallen under Cupid's old spell,
In Constantinople where they drive like hell.

Old friends say goodbye after lunch-time chat,
We wonder what we will all next be at.
Back to the office is the only sure thing,
Where money is earned so we can all do our thing.
See you soon, safe travels and don't work too hard,
Two kisses per cheek and we are all on the road.

TO BE

Sometimes it's hard to be apart

Sometimes it's hard to be brave
Sometimes it's hard to be cold
Sometimes it's hard to be daring
Sometimes it's hard to be early
Sometimes it's hard to be friends
Sometimes it's hard to be good
Sometimes it's hard to be happy
Sometimes it's hard to be in-love
Sometimes it's hard to be just
Sometimes it's hard to be kind
Sometimes it's hard to be lovely
Sometimes it's hard to be mellow
Sometimes it's hard to be nasty
Sometimes it's hard to be out
Sometimes it's hard to be poor
Sometimes it's hard to be quiet
Sometimes it's hard to be ready
Sometimes it's hard to be simple

Sometimes it's hard to be together

TELL ME ABOUT LOVE

I love you openly
But you cannot see this
Because you are looking
In the wrong direction
Just turn around now
And you will see.

I love you quietly
But you cannot hear this
Because you are listening
In the deafness of silence
Listen for our love now
And you will hear.

I love you completely
But you cannot feel this
Because we are touching
In sometimes sadness
Hold me closer now
And you will feel.

PARLAMI D'AMORE

Ti amo apertamente
ma tu non puoi vederlo
perchè stai guardando
nella direzione sbagliata
Voltati ora
e vedrai..

Ti amo quietamente
ma tu non puoi sentirlo
nel silenzio assordante
Ascolta il nostro amore ora
e sentirai.

Ti amo totalmente
ma tu non puoi sentirlo
perchè ci incontriamo
talvolta in momenti tristi
Tienimi vicino ora
e saprai

PARLE MOI D'AMOUR

Je t'aime ouvertement
Mais ça tu ne peux pas le voir
Parce que tu regardes
Dans la mauvaise direction
Tourne-toi à présent
Et tu verras.

Je t'aime discrètement
Mais ça tu ne peux pas l'entendre
Parce que tu écoutes
Dans la surdité du silence
Cherche notre amour à présent
Et tu l'entendras.

Je t'aime entièrement
Mais ça tu ne peux pas l'éprouver
Parce que nous nous touchons
Parfois dans la tristesse
Serre-moi plus fort à présent
Et tu le sentiras.

CUÉNTAME ACERA DEL AMOR

Yo te amo abiertamente
pero tu no puedes ver esto
por que tu estas buscando
en la dirección equivocada
solo dá la vuelta ahora
y tu verás.

te amo en silencio
pero tu no puedes oir esto
por que tu estas escuchando
en la sordera del silencio
escucha nuestro amor ahora
y tu oirás.

yo te amo completamente
pero tu no puedes sentir esto
por que tú estas tocando
algunas veces la tristeza
sosténme mas cera ahora
y tu sentirás.

WITHOUT

Like a car without a driver
Like a plane without a pilot
Like a boat without a captain

Like a town without a person
Like a hole without a space
Like a map without a place

Like a suit without a man
Like a shoe without a foot
Like a hat without a head

Like a cry without a child
Like a bark without a dog
Like a smile without a face

Like me

Without

You.

LOVE IS A DRUG

Addicted
To you.
I want
You now.
I need a fix,
I need to score.
The power of love,
The power of you,
My everything,
My heroine,
My heroin,
My mine,
My me,
You.
|
|
|
|
|
|

HAPPINESS

Is a million memories ...

Like your favourite Beatles track,
Like breakfast coffee in a Turin bar,
Like the old friends that never grow old,
Like your favourite Italian pasta in Rome,
Like summer swims in warm sea with cold rain,
Like the aria which sends shivers down your spine,
Like the magical taste of Gaja Barberesco for lunch,
Like coming home to a smiling face after a long trip,
Like your child buying you dinner for the first time,
Like how beautiful she was on your wedding day,
Like your first date movie being on TV again,
Like capturing a moment in a photograph,
Like rereading your favourite book,
Like watching Casablanca again,
Like publishing your first book,
Like living every moment...

... And a million more to come.

COMPLICATED & COMPLEX

Sophistication is the refuge of the complicated,
High maintenance, it's someone else's fault,
Infecting everyone with their little paranoias,
A black hole, taking all and giving nothing back.

Simple pleasures are the friends of the complex,
User-friendly, reliable and rather iPod-like,
Touching everyone with their magical dreams,
A desert oasis, giving all but getting even more.

WHO REALLY?

Twittering on Twitter with tweets,

Connecting to Facebook friends,

MySpaceing your music monthly,

Addicted to socializing socially,

Who really needs to network?

Switch off,

Tune in,

Simply be...

Quiet again.

ELECTION

The verbal diarrhoea of the politician's promises,
Rains on the broken roof of dripping umbrellas,
Hustings heckling hastening onset of pneumonia,
Voters need every candidate to be seen and heard.

Un-hygienic kissing of babies and pressing the flesh,
Flash avoiding fixed smile like toothpaste commercial,
Thinks - one man one vote a bad idea by Election Day,
I wonder does every candidate vote for themselves?

Tense wait as political pundits make newsless news,
Oscar-like performances as the winners are announced,
Four years in The Slough-of-Despond for the loser,
The Olympian heights of triumph for the winner.

IRISH SUMMER

Another sunless Irish Summer alas,
Not good for fair skinned cailín deas,
Who think to tan a lobster red is nice,
And SAD for the rest of us who will hate,
Three months daily sunless wetness,
All bored, bikini-less and beach-less.

Do something, do anything, do nothing,
Caged kids, grumpy adults, all moaning,
Weather our almost English obsession,
The legacy of 800 years of oppression,
So definitely we should start to read,
A sunshine picnic for the mind indeed.

THE LOOK

In a moment she catches my eye,
The glance, the quiet smile for me,
I know the look, it was all it took,
For Cupid's arrow to find it's mark.

Sometimes after breakfast coffee,
And maybe after lunchtime snack,
And often after romantic dinner,
She looks at me and then I know.

That life is good and we are right,
And all the problems of the light,
Will be put to rest in bed tonight,
With just a look my fears take flight.

LAST NIGHT

All through the night she keeps you awake.

Her skin so soft as she sleeps in your arms,
Her breath so quiet as you hold her tight,
Her scream of pleasure as you come as one,
Her body on fire as you climb the hill,
Her heart beats fast with rhythm of love,
Her gasps of pleasure as you slip inside,
Her lips so hot as you kiss her so hard,
Her breasts so perfect in the act of love,
Her desire so strong as you feel her wet,
Her passion so wild as she strips for you,
Her love so perfect as you look in her eyes,
Her beauty so radiant as she smiles hello.

All through the night you remember last night.

TONIGHT

In the darkness of this night,
Take my hand and hold it tight,
Caress me gently, touch my hair,
Just wanting you is hard to bear.

Kiss me now, our worlds collide,
Set free my passion deep inside,
Let me feel your heart beat fast,
Take away this pain at last.

Whisper soft those words of love,
Touch me, let your fingers rove,
To the place, we fly together,
Alone, together, each for other.

SKY

Familiar "Buenos dias" from Bianca again,
Sandwiched, betubed with 5000 miles to go,
The blue-black spaceness of the endless sky,
And runwayless earth of comfortable clouds,
Reflecting on what has been and is yet to come,
A million miles of poetry, pain and pleasure,
Star Trek on the TV, seared Tilapia on my plate,
Flying to you for a first-date hello-again feeling.

HOME

Home is
A feeling you get,
You don't need to fret,
When at ease in your mind,
You can just relax and unwind,
No need to live a life out loud,
You can be alone in a crowd,
At one with your heart,
In a place apart.
At home.

50

Being 50 you

should be glad,

100 would be

twice as bad.

WEARY

Weary worldwide,
Week three,
Travelling,tiring.

Worried waiting,
Wasted time,
Ticking, trapped.

Wishes wait,
Want, tender,
Touching, tomorrow.

Weekend welcome,
Will tease,
Thrilling, tonight.

Wake wise,
Wonderful, tea,
Toasting, together.

PAIN...

In love – is the absence of touch,
In hate – is the desire to be alone.

In fear – is the terror of not knowing,
In torture – is the need for an answer.

In war – is the waiting to fight,
In peace – is the settling of a difference.

In illness – is the need for a cure,
In death - is the tragedy of a loss.

In work – is the worry of termination,
In poverty – is the emptiness of hunger.

In wealth – is the stress of losing,
In gambling – is the blast of winning.

In you – is the absence of together,
In me – is the loneliness of travel.

.

WORKLESS

I am lonely, pink-slipped and home,
Wanted to be home but not like this,
I feel empty without my nine to five,
This other side looks different now.

Friends fear it's infectious and don't call,
Last week's empathy becomes sympathy,
Ex-colleagues simply have nothing to say,
Redundancy is the new invisibility cloak.

If you have a job, try to remember
To call all your workless friends,
A simple "Hello" won't kill you,
But the silence may kill them.

MEMORIES

Memories are

The building blocks

In the house of your life.

You can build a castle,

Or end up homeless.

Memories are

The rolling waves

On the beach of your life.

You can leave with barely a ripple

Or ride those waves.

ESPINADA

You lie in bed and close your eyes,
Your heart beats fast as you fantasise,
The restless feelings deep inside begin,
Hot as his fingers trace across your skin,
Over the hills and valleys his magic touch,
That exquisite burning fire you love so much,
Lips taste your passion wet musk perfume,
The urgent coaxing of the flower to bloom,
You lust on fire for him to take you over,
Thrust deep and bring you - oh so clever,
The thorns of pleasure - searing height,
As two are one and perfect is the night.

EYES WIDE SHUT

When I close my eyes and listen to
The thlunk of the fridge door,
The burble of water boiled,
The clink of a cup stirred,
The rasp of knife on toast,
The crispness of bacon frying,
The sweetness of butter melting,
The tartness of orange squeezed,
The closeness of breakfast for two,
The rustle of night-time silk,
I am where I love to be,
Close to you.

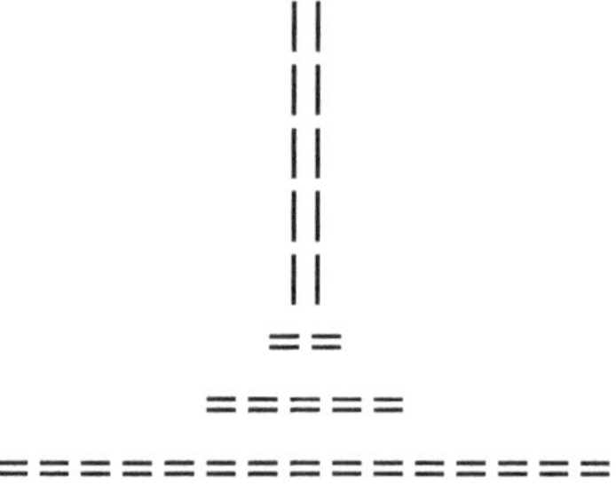

TIME TRAVEL

I was fifty-three this morning,
But I feel so much older now,
Having lived a lifetime in a day.

It started like a thousand others,
Time suddenly skipped a track,
Everyone I know is dead and gone-

I didn't even get to say goodbye.
I never knew that time was precious,
This morning was a hundred years ago.

BLACK OR WHITE

Today your sunrise is a cold black hole,
The sky-black emptiness burns you blind,
Blue doesn't care if you're black or white,
There's no drug to stop the pain of blue,
Tears are salt and blood is always red.

Tonight your night's a star-bright stage,
A silver spotlight laser-lights these words,
Blind before the poet works a magic spell,
Tomorrow sunrise red and sky clear blue,
Electric-sharp your new addiction's buzz.

Living your life in three dimension verse.

INSIDE OUT

I know that I loved you,
And more than a little,
But now you are gone.

I feel...

Too heartless to beat,
Too lonely to need,
Too empty to cry,
Too raw to bleed,
Too heavy to lie,
Too cold to be,
Too sad to try.

Please...

Come back to me now,
You are the love of my life,
The part of me missing.

SO LONG AGO

The loving look
Was all it took
To melt my heart,
My life to start,
So long ago.

Blossom blush,
Schoolgirl crush,
To take it slow,
We grew to know,
So long ago.

In midst of loving,
That 18 feeling,
When two are one,
And two were one,
So long ago.

NOTES

PICTURES

The picture on the front cover is of the Hilton Hotel in Madrid, the back cover is of an Auckland harbour sunrise, my portrait shot was taken in Schloss Dürnstein in Austria..

POEMS

ALAN – my special son with the rhythm of life

BLACK OR WHITE – the magic of poetry.

BLUE HORIZON – the hard edge of living in the air.

BUTTERFLIES FOR BREAKFAST? – almost never happens

CHISINAU – impressions of Moldova

COMPLEX & COMPLICATED – just some definitions

CUÉNTAME ACERA DEL AMOR – tell me about love

DROWNING IN YOUR EYES – waves of loving.

EL VIAJE FINAL - so many deaths on the road to Cochabamba whose lives were cut short - much to their surprise.

ELECTION – wanting and winning and losing

ESPINADA – the passion and the pleasure

EYES WIDE SHUT – taste what you hear

FATHER – semper fideles

FORGETTING – the mirror of remembering

GIVING – the rush after giving away everything

HAPPINESS – is those small big things in life

HILTON HOTEL – Madrid summer stopover

HOME – is a feeling not a place

IN VINO VERITAS – truth bullets in Cochabamba

INSIDE OUT – never let her go

IRISH SUMMER – another wet Irish Summer which should surprise nobody as that is why the fields are green

LAST NIGHT – you were with her, tonight she is gone

LAUNCH – a million impossible things before breakfast

LITTLE THINGS – those little things you do

LOVE IS DRUG – I am addicted to you

MAGIC MADRID – back again after twenty years

MEETING FOR LUNCH – impossible in 30 minutes.

MEMORIES - even if they live to be 100 some people's empty lives are very brief

PAIN – is part of living.

PARLAMI D'AMORE – tell me about love.

PARLE MOI DE AMOUR – tell me about love

PENNIES – try it – when you cut your finger – it tastes like the coins you licked when you were small.

PRISON – poetry can set you free from your personal prison.

RAIN – is never really wanted

REALITY TV – a dinner companion in Santo Domingo worried that her participation in a reality TV show the next week would not be a gourmet experience.

RED HOT SUMMER – a steaming hot cold shower.

REMEMBERING – the mirror of forgetting

SKY – flying home

SO LONG AGO – feeling 18 again.

SUICIDE – an unanswered cry for help requested by a perfectly logical mind.

SWEAT – cheese dreams

TELL ME ABOUT LOVE – absence lets the cracks in our love grow big – unless we really talk to each other.

TEMPTING – not to take this endless commute again to Bolivia mobile business and beyond.

THE FINAL JOURNEY – so many deaths on the road to Cochabamba, people whose lives were cut short - much to their surprise.

THE LOOK – that she gives you.

TIME AND DISTANCE – a growing relationship

TIME TRAVEL – did you ever feel that time was flying?

TO BE - apart and together again and the distance in-between

TONIGHT – together tonight

WEARY – home at the end of another long week

WHEN I DIE – celebrate my life

WHO REALLY? – your social addiction

WITHOUT - you

WORKLESS – but need a friend to call

50 –is only half way to 100

www.ingramcontent.com/pod-product-compliance
Ingram Content Group UK Ltd.
Pitfield, Milton Keynes, MK11 3LW, UK
UKHW041915190726
13854UKWH00003B/1260

9 781445 209616